THE HAYES BOOKS
DARING DEEDS

By
Teri Kelly
with
Stef Donev, Mary Kaizer Donev
and Dan Mackie

Editors:
Nadia Pelowich
Paul Hayes
Curtis Rush

Designed and Illustrated by
Denis Gagne

Penworthy Publishing Company, 219 North Milwaukee St., Milwaukee, Wisconsin 53202
Printed in Hong Kong

Copyright 1986 by Hayes Publishing Ltd.

ISBN 0-87617-025-4
Printed in Hong Kong

CONTENTS

Remember the Alamo

In the heart of San Antonio, Texas, stand the worn and weathered walls of a fortress. The Alamo, as it is called, is visited annually by thousands - it is a museum. It is also a symbol; more than housing relics of days gone by, it holds the memory and spirit of a daring few who, until the end, challenged defeat.

More than a hundred years ago, in 1836 - when Texas still belonged to Mexico - a small band of men, women, and children made their way to San Antonio. So that they would no longer have to pay taxes to Mexico, so that Texas would gain its freedom, this band of volunteers was willing to fight. Led by Colonel William B. Travis, an Alabama lawyer, they were the "army" of General Sam Houston, leader of the Texas Freedom Fighters. Their mission: to occupy the Alamo fortress and from there, to keep back the Mexican army.

The band of 188 Texas freedom fighters took their positions within the Alamo walls. They'd been joined by two legendary American pioneers, Colonel David Crockett and Colonel Jim Bowie, both known for their bravery and fighting skills. Even with these two American heroes, however, their chances were slim.

When the Mexican army came into view, those behind the Alamo walls realized they were outnumbered 10 to 1. The Mexican troops surrounded the fortress, their uniforms and swords glittering in the sun. There were thousands of them! Waving a white flag, one of their messengers rode up to the Alamo on horseback. The Mexicans were giving them one chance to surrender. Colonel Travis answered with a cannon shot. The Battle of the Alamo was begun!

The Mexicans were bombarding the Alamo around the clock but the cannons were too small and the fortress walls too strong - the siege of the Alamo would not be as easy as the Mexicans first thought. During one of the rifle volleys, however, Colonel Travis was seriously wounded.

Commanding from his cot, Travis learned that reinforcements would not be arriving in time. To stay at the Alamo and fight would mean certain death! Travis called all the people in the mission together and etched a line in the sand with his sword. He announced that he would be remaining at the Alamo to fight to the death and that any who wished to remain and fight by his side, should cross the line. All others were free to leave.

At first, only a few crossed the line, and then a few more, until all the freedom fighters except one had crossed the line and voted to fight to the death.

For almost two weeks the small, weary Texans held out against the large Mexican troop. The Mexicans had no idea that the size of the Texan army was so small. Cannon and rifle shots were fired constantly, giving the Mexicans the idea that the Alamo was manned by thousands rather than under 200.

Finally, at daybreak on March 6, 1836, the Mexicans' bugles and bands played *El Deguello,* ancient Spanish fighting music. It meant, "Beheading, cutting the throat...no mercy to every opponent." The Mexican army stormed the walls of the Alamo. Armed with axes, scaling ladders, and knives and rifles, they breached the walls and swarmed inside the fortress.

The Texans defended the Alamo in vicious hand-to-hand combat. From room to room of the convent building and in the chapel of the mission, the fighting continued until all the defenders were dead.

When General Sam Houston received the news of the massacre, he was enraged. At four in the afternoon of April 21, 1836, he and 900 men swept across the prairie, hungry for revenge. Galloping full force on horseback, and howling, "Remember the Alamo! Remember the Alamo!" they swooped down upon the Mexican army.

Most of the Mexicans were killed, wounded or captured in the battle. The Mexican president was captured the next day. Under the terms of a treaty made at Velasco on May 14, 1836, Mexico agreed to recognize the independence of Texas and to withdraw its borders beyond the Rio Grande.

HIGH DIVERS OF MEXICO

From the ground Raul Garcia appears as a tiny silhouette against the sky. Standing erect on the rock known as *La Quebrada* in Acapulco, Mexico, he is deep in concentration. In just moments he will dive 118 feet into waters little deeper than twice his height. To do this he must first leap 27 feet in the air to clear the rocks below which extend 21 feet from the cliff's base.

With every muscle taut with exertion, Raul lunges skyward. Then, gracefully curving his body downward, he splashes to his target amid the wild cheers of his audience.

Raul Garcia and his team of 27 expert divers perform these dives regularly for their living. They belong to an exclusive club known as "Club de Clavadistas," or "club of high divers." Raul alone has made more than 35,000 dives!

SIX ANGELS TO FREEDOM

When the first world aerobatics championships were held in Czechoslovakia in 1960, the winner, Ladislav Bezak (known as Ladi by the American competitors) surprised everyone. Only military and test pilots in Czechoslovakia were known to have the necessary experience to be in competitions, and Ladi was only a university student!

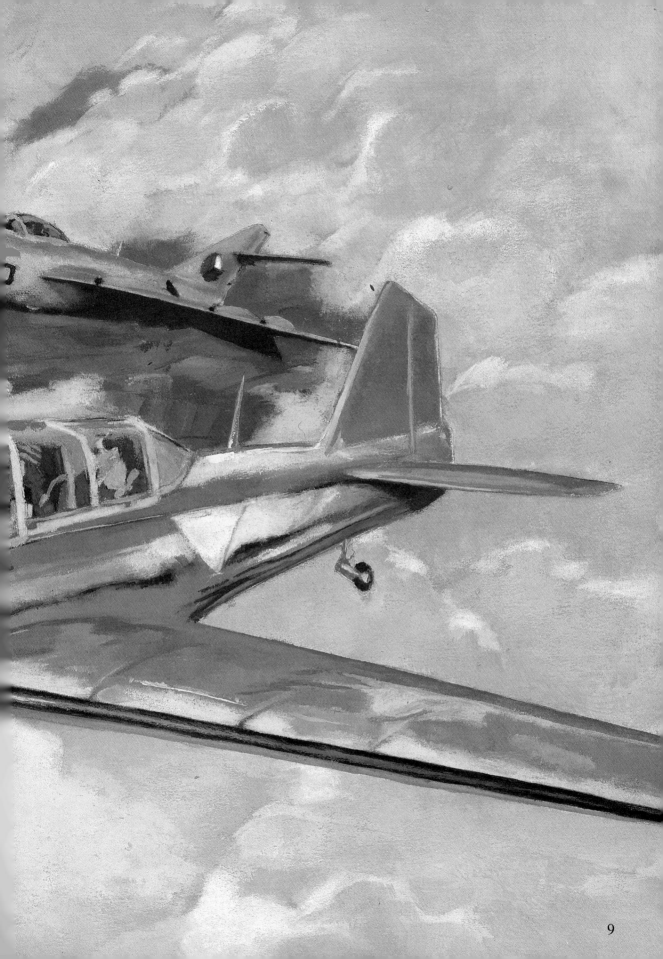

As a World Champion, Ladi earned a job at the Central School for Air Cadets, and compared to the average Czech citizen, he had great freedom - often he traveled to the west, both with the Czech airlines and as an air show pilot and competitor. Ladi's friendliness with the Westerners did not go unnoticed. The seeds of freedom had been sown - Ladi wanted to escape the communist government of his country - and Czech authorities watched Ladi with suspicion.

Although it was illegal for private persons to own their own airplane, it was not illegal for them to buy aircraft parts, and so he did. Little by little, Ladi collected the pieces to build his own airplane, but, after the Russian invasion of 1968, laws became stricter. It was now illegal for Ladi to buy gasoline for his plane, and though the danger of being found out was a constant threat, he got by with trading parts and favors for fuel.

On December 18, 1971, Ladi proposed his defection plan to his wife, Marie.

"When?" she asked.

"Right away," he replied. The security forces were steadily growing stronger and they could not afford to wait.

Marie took the children to a farm. At the first light of day, Ladi arrived, landing in the fields nearby. Fitting five people into the single front seat of the airplane was a problem, but not their greatest. Although it was December, a heat wave had swept the country, turning the frozen ground into a sea of mud. Twice, the airplane ran down the field, but with the extra weight, the mud was just too deep to lift off.

Ladi unloaded his family. Marie was to take the children to some trees near the end of the airport where he worked. There, they would hide and wait.

Even without his family, Ladi found taking off difficult. He barely made it over the trees when a thought occurred to him: what if someone back at the airport noticed the mud on his wheels? It was a state crime to land in a farmer's field and if they found out, his plane would be suspected.

But nobody spotted the mud. Ladi waited until noon when the airport staff would all be at lunch. Then, getting into his plane, he taxied to the end of the runway, praying that his wife and children would not be seen running from their hiding place in the trees to cram into the front cockpit once again.

With everyone packed in, the plane felt as heavy as a giant slug. Ladi gulped with uncertainty, but, after nearly a one-mile take off run, his Zlin 226 finally staggered into the air.

He flew north for a few minutes so as not to arouse the suspicion of radar operators - then he turned west. Within five minutes, there was a Russian-built MIG 17 jet fighter at his side. Seeing that Ladi was not going to respond to its warning, it pulled away but moments later machine gun tracer bullets went by - a final warning. The MIG passed by again, then circled around behind him, once more into an attack position.

If the MIG pilot was one of the regular Czech Air Force pilots, Ladi knew that he had a good chance, but if the pilot was an instructor, the Bezak family were in big trouble.

As the MIG closed in, ready to fire, Ladi started into a forward loop, knowing the MIG would be flying too fast to follow. He prayed his airplane would not go out of control because of the extra load and imbalance. Again, tracers went by, but the bullets were wide. When the MIG attacked a final time Ladi did an abrupt maneuver to avoid the bullets, knowing that sooner or later the MIG would find its mark. In desperation, he climbed and flew into the clouds.

After flying for nearly an hour, he saw houses through a hole in the cloud. Austria!

He climbed up to 6,000 feet and radioed "Here we come — six angels flying to freedom!"

10

THE FLYING WALLENDAS

Every seat in Madison Square Gardens in New York City was filled. It was 1928 and people had come from all over to see the German troupe known as "The Flying Wallendas." The troupe was to perform the death-defying and most exciting circus act ever. Without the precaution of a safety net below them, the Wallendas would attempt a bicycle ride on high wires at a height of 70 feet!

It was advertised that the Wallendas would form a human pyramid while riding bicycles over the high wire. Two of the brothers, Joseph and Herman, would pedal their bicycles one in front of the other with a long pole connecting them. A third brother, Karl, would sit on a chair that was balanced on the pole held by Joseph and Herman. As if this were not enough, their sister, Helen, would stand with outstretched arms, balancing herself on Karl's shoulders!

In their positions, the Wallendas proceeded to cross the wire. One slight slip could mean instant death for this family. Finally, the Wallendas reached the safety scaffold. The crowd broke into a thunderous roar that lasted 15 minutes!

In 1962, before a crowd of 6,000 in Detroit Michigan, the famous human pyramid crumbled and two of the Wallendas fell 36 feet to their death.

OMAHA BEACH

Known as "Operation Overlord," the D-day invasion would have to take place on one of three days in June - the 5th, 6th, or 7th. According to meteorological studies, two of the most important weather requirements could be expected for Normandy, France, on those three days - a late rising moon, and shortly after dawn, a low tide.

The paratroopers and airborne troops especially needed the moonlight, but because this was a surprise attack, they needed darkness until they arrived over the dropping zones. The naval troops needed a low tide to expose the millions of land mines which had been planted on the beach.

Rank after rank of mighty British ships approached the beaches. Around midnight of June 6th, 120 paratroopers landed in Normandy. Their mission was to mark "drop zones" for the full-scale American airborne assault that would begin at 1:15 a.m.

Glider planes swooped down, shocking the unprepared Germans. The first part of the D-Day battle was over within 15 minutes. The Germans were so confused by the attack, they were still not sure how many men had landed, whether it was a real invasion, or merely a French underground attack. No one was willing to sound the alarm for fear they would be wrong.

By 5:50 a.m., the American 1st Infantry, under the command of Omar N. Bradley, made their way onto Omaha Beach. Three thousand men were leading the attack. They didn't know, however, that the enemy was prepared. German Major Werner Pluskat's headquarters on Omaha Beach had been shelled, but unknown to the Americans, his men had survived.

The American troops were just one mile, or fifteen minutes, from shore. Why, they wondered, was it so silent?

As the first landing boats came to about 400 yards from shore, the enemy's guns opened fire. Shocked, the Americans jumped from their boats to wade waist-deep toward shore. The "Bloody Omaha" battle had begun.

Heavy fire from enemy guns stormed upon the waiting men. From high atop cliff walls German guns blasted down upon the beach. Those who had leapt over the sides of the landing boats to make their way to the shore were greeted by machine-gun fire. They were never able to raise their own guns in defense. Others drowned before reaching shore, dragged down under by the weight of their heavy gear.

Those who survived the shelling took refuge behind enemy obstacles positioned in the water. They had one mission - to cross 200 yards of enemy land mines and obstacles strewn along the shore, climb the hillside and take shelter behind a sea wall. This would be next to impossible. The machine-gun fire was incessant. There was no cover along the sand and, weighted down by their heavy equipment, the American troops moved sluggishly.

Misfortune mounted. A high wind that evening forced many boats off course. By nightfall, American casualties would mount to 50 percent.

By 7:00 a.m. the second wave of ships approached the wreckage known as Omaha Beach. Dead soldiers were strewn along every mile. Medics approaching shore to help the injured didn't know where to begin. The third and fourth waves came in. They too were shocked to see such devastation and even more surprised to see enemy fire. They had assumed that by now, all enemy guns would have been seized. The invasion was a near disaster! The first encouraging news came at 11:00 a.m. By early afternoon General Bradley knew that they were finally gaining ground. About 1:30 p.m., V corps aboard the *Augusta* relieved the gun-weary 1st Infantry. The situation on the beach slowly improved. Regimental staff were sent along the shores to reorganize troops. Then, a new attack was launched.

The American tanks fired. The enemy's reinforced concrete walls shook and crumbled. In what was one of the bloodiest battles German defenders were forced to surrender.

Now that the Atlantic Wall had been breached the Allies pushed inland to complete their D Day objectives - to reclaim Europe!

DOUGLAS BADER

Douglas Bader could fly with the best, and his aim was accurate. Movement on land, however, required something extra - persistence.

During a raid in August, 1941, a German plane ran into the tail of Bader's plane. As he tried to jump, one of his artificial legs caught in the cockpit cover. He fell thousands of feet before he worked his way free, but finally, he was able to open his parachute. He landed safely, but with two broken ribs.

When the Germans captured him the legend of the "legless fighter pilot" was so well-known to them that they treated him as an honored guest, instead of as a prisoner. They even broadcast a message to England, requesting that Bader's spare legs be airlifted to him so he could use them while he was a prisoner of war. As soon as Bader had his new leg, parachuted to him by a British plane flying over under a flag of truce, he climbed down a rope of bed sheets out of his second floor hospital window and escaped! When the Germans finally caught him, they were so furious they immediately sent him to a POW camp.

That didn't stop Bader. He made several more escape attempts, once disguising himself as part of an outside working party near an airport. He hoped to steal a plane. His plan was discovered, however, and this time, Bader was sent to Colditz fortress, known for its impenetrable security. To further ensure that Bader would not escape, they took away his artificial legs every night.

Bader was in Colditz until the U.S. Army liberated the camp in April of 1945.

LITTLE SURE SHOT

Her schoolmates nicknamed her "Moses Poses" but she would become known to the world as Annie Oakley, the Little Sure Shot from the West.

Born as Phoebe Ann Moses, Annie was the fifth child of a very poor family. At the age of 5, when Annie's father died, leaving her mother without means to support herself and her children, Annie was sent to an orphanage. Her stay there was cruel and punishing. Abused by her schoolmasters, she learned soon to be tough. Annie's letters of help addressed to her mother were destroyed by the teachers and Annie realized she was on her own. Her destiny was in her own hands, and so, in the still of the night, Annie escaped.

Returning home, she found her mother remarried but no richer than before. Her new stepfather was even less supportive than the father who had died, and Annie, determined to raise herself and her starving family above the poverty line, shouldered her rifle and disappeared into the woods. That evening she returned laden with wild game.

In Annie's time, around the late 1800's, hunting wild animals for food was considered a normal part of life. Not only did Annie hunt to supply her family's supper table, but being so accurate a shot, she successfully bagged quail and grouse to sell to the shopkeepers and hotel owners in the city. Annie was given a regular job by these merchants to keep them stocked with wild game. Needless to say, Annie's family was overjoyed with her resourcefulness, and with the extra income they were able to pay off the mortgage on their home. Her skill had raised her above the poverty line, as she'd intended - she had no idea it would raise her to the heights of world wide fame.

While still a young girl, Annie visited a shooting gallery in town. She shot off six wooden ducks so quickly, it stunned the onlookers. In disbelief, they asked her to try it again, and once more Annie shot down the wooden ducks. The audience was astounded!

The owners of the gallery introduced Annie to a famous sharpshooter named Frank Butler, who was visiting in town. They bet Butler $50.00 that Annie could out-shoot him. The

targets were to be clay discs fired into the air by a powerful spring.

Frank Butler fired first as the clay disc was sent whirling through the air. It shattered into a dozen black pieces. Now it was Annie's turn. Again the black disc went hurling into the air. Annie raised her rifle and blasted the disc to bits. They each, in turn, successfully shot 24 clay discs. Butler's 25th disc was released into the air. He aimed his rifle. A loud blast was heard - but the clay disc was still intact, falling rapidly to the ground. Annie quickly lifted her rifle, rested the butt end on her shoulder, took aim, and demolished Butler's clay disc before it hit the ground. Young Annie won the match against a professional marksman!

Butler was intrigued by Annie's abilities. He made himself a regular guest at Annie's home and later they were married. Annie and Frank were booked together on a theatrical tour and were well accepted by audiences everywhere. The public fell in love with this young sharp shooter, so Frank decided to devote his energies to becoming her manager and assistant.

Annie joined *Buffalo Bill's* Wild West Show which featured such celebrities as Chief Sitting Bull, leader of the Indians at the Battle of Little Bighorn. He nicknamed Annie "Little Sure Shot." Even among these popular performers, Annie instantly became the star attraction. Newspapers called her "The Little Girl of the Western Plains."

For her performance, Annie would ride in on a spotted pony. She wore a flowered deerskin jacket and skirt. She rode quickly and confidently, shooting down targets one after another as a nearby rider tossed the targets through the air. She daringly extinguished the flames of revolving candles while standing upside down on horseback! In another stunt she leaped from her horse to the floor of the ring, reached for a rifle from a gun stand, then quickly shot down five glass balls tossed to her by Frank. Her act included a spinning glass ball attached to a string. Annie, using only a mirror to view her target, would shoot the glass ball, shattering it into a million tiny pieces. She shot dimes spinning in Frank's fingers, and shot cigarettes from Frank's mouth. The audiences loved it! Never before had audiences anywhere seen such wonders from such a small, young woman.

Annie had reached the big time! She and Frank and the Wild Wild West Show traveled to Europe to perform before Queen Victoria, who was celebrating her Golden Jubilee. Annie also performed for Emperor Wilhelm I of Germany. The Crown Prince of Germany took Frank's place in the show, demanding that Annie shoot a lighted cigarette that was held between his lips. The audience was aghast! What if she missed! The tension was thick. The Crown Prince stood sideways a fair distance from Annie. Confidently, she raised her rifle to her shoulder while everyone held their breath, and with one swift blast, she extinguished the cigarette.

Annie's next step was the movies. With Buffalo Bill, Annie met with Thomas Edison, inventor of, among other things, the kinetograph - an early type of movie camera. Annie performed a pantomime exhibiting her shooting talents. The "Silent Screen" was, at that time, the most popular form of entertainment.

Annie continued to thrill audiences for over 30 years. Even as she moved on to old age she retained the quick reactions that made her a world-class sharpshooter.

At the age of 66, November 3, 1926, Annie died in her sleep. Her husband Frank was so depressed at the passing of "his little girl" that exactly 20 days later, he died and was buried next to her in Brock, Ohio. The famous entertainer and newspaper columnist, Will Rogers, wrote this tribute to Annie Oakley:

"She was the acknowledged headliner for years in the great Buffalo Bill Show; the best known woman in the world at one time, for when she was with the show, it toured everywhere. She was not only the greatest rifle shot for a woman that ever lived, but I doubt if her character could be matched anywhere outside of a saint…."

CHUCK YEAGER

Scientists were convinced that U. S. Air Captain, Chuck Yeager was on a suicide mission. If that wasn't enough, it was made worse by the fact that, unknown to anyone but his friend Captain Jack Ridley, Yeager was flying the mission with two broken ribs. The intense pain weakened his right arm so that it was almost useless. Without a piece of broomhandle that his friend had smuggled into the craft for him, he couldn't even close the hatch on his experimental X-1 rocket plane.

No machine had ever gone faster than the speed of sound, 738 miles per hour. Every time the experimental rocket planes got near the speed of sound - also called Mach One - they rattled and shook so violently that the pilots and scientists feared they would disintegrate in the air.

Many scientists were sure that nothing - and no one - could survive breaking the sound barrier. Still, America held the hope of one day putting men and women into space, and such a feat required that airships travel faster than the speed of sound. If the sound barrier could not be broken, mankind could never reach outer space.

Yeager wanted to be the first man to do it. He knew that if he'd told anyone about the two broken ribs, they would have picked another pilot for the mission. Yeager couldn't allow that - it was now or never.

The Air Force pilot had broken his ribs while horseback riding through the desert with his wife. A civilian doctor had examined and bandaged them, advising Yeager not to do anything strenuous for the next few weeks. Yet, it was only the next morning that Yeager strapped himself into the plane using the broom-handle to secure the hatch from the inside.

On the morning of October 14, 1947, as he flew over the California desert, the World War II veteran fighter pilot forced himself to ignore the pain. Concentrating, he forgot the broken ribs and thought only about his job and his plane. He had the skill, he was confident in his own abilities and he was convinced that his plane, the Glamorous Glennis - named after his wife - could succeed in the mission.

The Glamorous Glennis was really little more than a winged tube with four giant rockets stuffed inside it. In fact, Yeager and the plane were being carried aloft in the bomb bay of a B-29 bomber. When the plane reached 29,000 feet, it would be "bombs away," and Yeager and his X-1 would drop down.

As the X-1 dropped through space, Yeager started the four rockets, one by one. The plane shook and rattled violently and Yeager was tossed about inside. The controls wouldn't respond properly and his goggles clouded. He could barely read the dials which showed his speed. Then, though it continued to shake, the plane seemed to stay at Mach .98, just below the speed of sound. It refused to be pushed beyond that limit.

Finally...the gauge shot past Mach One. The shaking stopped. Yeager felt the plane steady and the ride became calm, smooth - and silent. The sound was behind him as he raced ahead of it. It couldn't keep up with him. Yeager was flying faster than even sound could travel.

The space age had begun.

First Free Fall Parachute

Georgina Thompson, or "Tiny Broadwick" as she became known, wondered what it would be like to jump from an airplane.

Already a wife and mother at the tender age of 15, she joined the Charles Broadwick stunt parachute team in 1908 hoping to realize her dream. She soon discovered firsthand, the euphoric feeling of leaping from an aircraft and drifting silently through the clouds.

From a homemade biplane that took her over Griffith Park in Los Angeles, Tiny made her first jump on June 21, 1913. Such jumps had been made before, however, and because the parachute opened automatically the parachutist had little to worry about but landing properly. What had never been done was a "free fall jump" - where the rip cord is pulled manually by the parachutist. In this kind of jump, all kinds of things could go wrong. The parachutist could pull the rip cord too soon and get the chute caught up in the plane, or if the cord was pulled too late, the parachutist might already be going too fast for a safe landing.

The next year, in 1914, Tiny volunteered and succeeded in becoming the first person to do a free fall jump.

Queen of the Channel

The frigid waters crashed against the rocks with waves climbing 10 feet high. The dark sky was like the inside of a cave, with only the moon for a lantern, as Cindy Nicholas slipped into Lake Ontario at Youngstown, New York, just four days before her 17th birthday. Her struggle with nature would be cruel and punishing. This was Cindy's first marathon swim. On August 16, 1974, after 15 hours and 10 minutes of constant battle with the elements, Cindy emerged victorious at Ontario Place, in Toronto, Canada. She had set an all-time record for both men and women for the Lake Ontario crossing.

A competitive, determined young woman, Cindy explained, "The channel was the natural follow-up. If you're to be considered a marathon swimmer, as such, you swim the English Channel."

The winter prior to the English Channel crossing was spent in constant preparation. The training was similar to that of a marathon runner. Cindy swam six to ten miles at a time in an indoor pool until she was at the peak of her physical and mental condition.

On July 29, 1975, the great moment had arrived. Cindy took to the waters of the English Channel from the shores of France. Once again placing herself at the mercy of nature, Cindy took on the challenge with vigor and confidence. Her only companion in this dark, lonely trek through hostile waters was the pilot boat operator, who stayed with her every stroke of the way. Cindy completed her swim to the shores of England in a record time of 9 hours, 46 minutes. This success, however, did not mark the end of her conquests.

During the summer of her historic English Channel swim, she traveled to Syria where she swam the oil-drenched 15 mile crossing from Jabul to Katakia - the first woman to achieve this goal. The following year when the attention of sports enthusiasts the world over was turned to the Montreal Olympics, Cindy swam the English Channel, not once, but twice! She swam from England to France in 10 hours, 20 minutes on September 6, and eleven days later returned to England in nearly the same time. Cindy was preparing for her greatest challenge yet - a round-trip swim across the English Channel!

Cindy thought she had known all the agony marathon swimming had to offer. She had never known, though, the painful, weakening stings of the jelly fish. Soon after she dived in to begin the round trip crossing, intense pain forced her to stop.

So damaging were the stings that she was unable to raise her arm properly for four days after her last channel swim. As a result of this attempted swim she suffered chronic neck inflammation resembling the symptoms of arthritis; one neurosurgeon predicted she would never swim a marathon again.

But Cindy refused to stop. She consulted with other neurosurgeons until she discovered one who would help her through her affliction. Under doctor's care and with proper medication, Cindy continued swimming. To prove to herself and the world that she would not be beaten, Cindy crossed Chaleur Bay (in New Brunswick) to Quebec, achieving distinction as the first woman ever to do so.

Only one month after the Chaleur Bay crossing, Cindy returned to the English Channel. The two-way crossing had yet to be done.

The following year, as the winds howled furiously, Cindy plunged into the black waters from the shores of England. In 8 hours, 55 minutes, beating the previous record by two minutes, she reached French soil. The return trip to England would not be as easy as the first leg of the journey.

Upon leaving the French shoreline, she was thrust against the rocks by huge waves. She struggled to get back on course but the turmoil of the waters sapped her energy. Minutes passed as she sank from sight, and then resurfaced, bobbing above the waves with legs bashed, bruised and bleeding. Coating her legs first with Vaseline. Cindy dived into the frothing horizon. Eleven hours later she touched England's shore only 10 yards from when she had departed. This two-way crossing set a record of 19 hours, 55 minutes - an incredible 10 hours less than the previous record!

During her career, Cindy had set and broken numerous records, always returning to meet the perils of marathon swimming when others, less determined, would have hung up the swimsuit and retired. Facing her challenge with stubborn tenacity, Cindy crossed the English Channel 10 times in her swimming career - appropriately, she earned the title "Queen of the Channel."

A QUEST FOR FAME

Annie Taylor, a widowed, childless, 43-year-old school teacher craved a change in her quiet life. She wanted recognition, fame and adventure, and she was willing to risk her life for it. Annie was going to attempt to drop over the Horseshoe Falls in a barrel!

On October 24, 1901, she made a striking appearance through the cheering crowd, her massive form clad in a black, flowing gown and floppy hat. Discreetly, for she was a shy woman, she changed from her formal dress into a short skirt, which was in itself a major feat of courage, considering the Victorian modesty of her times.

Before climbing into the barrel, Annie turned to the crowd and waved, "Au revoir. I'll not say good-bye because I'm coming back."

Annie was transported to nearby Grass Island, where she was lowered into the wooden barrel. Bound by seven hoops, the barrel measured four and a half feet high by four feet in diameter and was exactly the same weight as Annie - 160 pounds! She was then taken by rowboat to where the currents were strong. A 100 pound anvil was secured to the barrel's bottom to keep it upright as it floated.

As the barrel drifted toward the Falls the crowd held its breath. The barrel tossed and flipped, then finally bounced over the Falls while, inside, Annie braced herself. Crashing to the bottom, the barrel bobbed and drifted as, almost immediately, waiting rescuers fished her from the water, safe and sound.

THE DAM BUSTERS

It was in May during the early stages of World War II. Barnes Wallis, a British scientist and engineer, paced the floor, a worried expression on his face. He had not slept properly for the past few days, waiting and fearing this very hour. Three flights of Lancaster bombers were making raids on dams in Germany, using a special bomb that Wallis had invented. The raid itself required extraordinary courage and daring. But what if his invention didn't work?

Barnes Wallis knew that if the large dams in Germany could be broken, it would cripple the hydroelectric power and water supply that served a multitude of factories which produced ammunition, airplanes, and equipment. That is not to mention the destruction that would be caused by the flood of water that would charge down the valleys, wrecking everything in its path!

Destroying the dams, however, was not an easy task. Built of concrete and earth a hundred feet thick, the dams were impenetrable to bombs. Even a direct hit would not damage them. As well, they were protected by a torpedo net, and so a completely new approach had to be taken.

Wallis developed his plan. He had read in some old construction records that, sometimes, even a relatively small charge placed deep in the water next to a structure could do a surprising amount of damage.

Wallis designed a barrel-shaped bomb that hung under the planes, and the planes were rigged with a motor system to set the barrels spinning. The idea was that if the bombs were dropped just right they'd skip like skipping stones, right over the torpedo net, hit the dam, sink to the bottom and then explode, destroying the dam.

To make the plan work in Germany, Wallis's bomb would have to be dropped at precisely sixty feet off the water - not much higher than a five-story building. To escape detection, the plan would have to be carried out at night and there were no instruments to measure height that accurately. A solution was found: by mounting two lights on an airplane, two light spots showed on the ground. As the airplane lowered, the light spots on the ground would grow closer together - when these spots touched, the pilot knew he was at the right height.

The question of how to measure the right distance from the dams was another matter, but simple geometry produced the answer. As each of the dams had turrets that were exactly 600 feet apart, a simple bombsight was made out of a piece of plywood with a peephole at one end and two nails sticking up at the other. By looking through the peephole, the bombardier merely had to line up the two nails with the turrets.

Three dams would be attacked at the same time - during a moonlit night in May, when the dams would be full of water from the spring runoff.

Nineteen Lancaster bombers were used. Nine of them would be sent to the Moehne dam, and if that was successful, they would go on to the Eder dam. Five aircraft would attack the Sorpe dam, and five more would take off later as a reserve formation.

As they approached the Dutch coast, German flak from antiaircraft guns came up. Little orange flashes filled the sky all around them. One aircraft got hit, knocking out its radios, so it had to turn back. Another Lancaster lowered itself to sixty feet over the Zuyder Zee - a body of water in Holland - to try its lights. One of the lights failed, and it hit the water, tearing the bomb off and scooping up so much water that the gunner nearly drowned. That bomber too, had to turn back. Two more aircraft were caught by flak, and crashed. They had not even reached their target and already four of the nine aircraft were down.

As they attacked the Moehne, tracers flashed at them from the turrets on the dam. One bomb dropped, but the dam still stood. Another bomber was hit by gunfire, and its bomb skipped right over the dam, exploding harmlessly below. Two more bombs were dropped and each time a huge wave of water washed over the top, but still the dam stood. Finally, after a third hit, the dam split.

Water roared through a ragged hole a hundred feet deep and a hundred feet wide. Wallis received the code word by radio and jumped around like an excited child. Soon two other code words would be broadcast and the message relayed to him. Success! All three dams had been breached.

30

BURIED ALIVE!

Coffins and burial are usually associated with death but for Mrs. Emma Smith, burial meant a test of courage, endurance and self-reliance.

The 38-year-old mother of three from Nottinghamshire, England, wanted to beat the record held by an Irishman who had stayed underground for 61 days. To do this, Emma Smith would be buried alive for 100 days! Her 8-foot coffin was to be covered with 10 tons of dirt!

This was no ordinary satin-lined coffin, however. Equipped with electric lights and heating, it had a pipe connecting the coffin to the surface which provided her with food and drink, and a closed-circuit TV which allowed nurses to view Emma around the clock to ensure her safety. A radiotelephone was installed and Mrs. Smith could communicate daily with her family.

To avoid boredom, Emma wrote letters to her friends and knitted sweaters for her family. She also kept a journal of her experience in the coffin which was later published by a local newspaper.

On September 17, 1968, after 101 days in her coffin, Emma Smith emerged victorious and relieved to be on the surface again!

Houdini - Master of Escape

Harry Houdini's secret to his incredible escape act still remains a mystery. Audiences the world over believed Houdini to have supernatural powers. Baffled by his underwater escape trick - the "Challenge to Death," later known as his "Water Torture Cell Stunt" - onlookers had no way of explaining his survival. Even less could they explain what would drive a man to defy death every day of his life.

Born as Ehrich Wess, Houdini was a precocious child, fascinated by the mysterious and unknown. When the circus came to town, he would carefully examine the tricks performed by magicians and trapeze artists. At the age of 9 he charged admission to his own circus in his backyard in Milwaukee, Wisconsin. Swinging through the air on a makeshift trapeze that was attached to a tree, he'd suspend himself by his feet and pick objects from the ground with his teeth. The stage was set: the greatest magician of history was already practicing his profession.

Ehrich's appetite for magic was not lost with the coming of adulthood. The volumes of books he read on the subject only increased his hunger for yet more knowledge, and countless hours were spent studying the stunts and techniques of the greatest in the field. Two magicians who most impressed him were the Frenchman, Jean Eugene Robert-Houdin, and the American, Harry Keller, who was noted for his escape tricks. Ehrich's dream was to one day reach their level of expertise and fame.

In 1888, at age 17, Ehrich decided to make his fortune in New York City. By combining the names of his heroes, Harry Keller and Robert-Houdin, he became "Harry Houdini." A name was easy enough to change; the success that he hoped would go with it, however, would be long in coming. With his fumbling brother, Theo, as his assistant, Harry was, at times, even booed off the stage.

Harry researched and studied every kind of lock and how to open it. He learned how to open locks, or "pick" them, without using keys. In one performance, he had himself locked and shackled inside an authentic prison cell. Within eight minutes he was free from his chains and standing on the outside of the cell! But New York was still not impressed.

Discouraged, Harry journeyed to Europe with his wife, Bess. His plan was to make the headlines of Europe - then, perhaps New York would take notice of him.

The plan worked. Harry's popularity spread quickly throughout Europe until soon he was known as "The Great Houdini." Although some people publicly challenged his escape act, others tried to imitate it. This infuriated Harry. To avoid being imitated he had to develop an act so great, so extraordinary, that it could not be copied.

His new escape trick included gymnastics and athletic skill. With his wrists handcuffed, he plunged into an enormous milk can that was filled with water. An assistant placed the top on the milk can and locked it with 6 padlocks. The audience was asked to hold its breath for however long it could. After about 30 seconds the audience heaved for air but Harry was still locked inside the water filled can! The audience squirmed with terror. Three minutes lapsed, when finally Harry emerged from the can dripping wet and smiling from ear to ear.

Harry improved on this act! Instead of merely plunging himself inside a water-filled can, he now had himself and the can lowered into the river - and still he emerged unscathed!

At last, New York beckoned. The year was 1904 and Harry, earning a salary of $1,000 a week, was at the height of his fame. To amaze the American audience and to capture the newspaper headlines, Harry planned an extraordinary feat. He would escape from the same prison cell that once held the murderer of President James A. Garfield. Then, he would unlock all the doors in the jail and rearrange the prisoners in different cells.

The act was a great success! The publicity was enormous! Harry was now in great demand and expanded his interests to the film industry, became president of his own film company - the "Houdini Picture Corporation" - and wrote books on the ways of his magic.

Reaching the level of greatness that he had did not stop Harry from improving his act. Learning to fly just 6 years after the Wright brothers made their first attempt at flying. Harry performed daredevil stunts in the sky. To improve his water escape act he practiced breathing to the extent that he did not appear to need air for nearly two hours. He trained with weights to strengthen his stomach muscles and challenged people to punch his stomach to show his audiences the greatness of his strength. No one could imitate the Great Houdini now.

At a performance at McGill University in Montreal, Canada, Houdini challenged a young student to test the strength of his stomach muscles. However, before Harry could tense himself to prepare for the attack, the student delivered three swift blows to his abdomen. Later that evening, Harry was in great pain but, saying nothing of it, went on to a performance in Detroit the next day. There, with all eyes upon him, Harry dropped to the floor partway through his act.

Harry Houdini died on October 31, 1926 - Hallowe'en night - of a ruptured appendix. In his will he requested to be buried in a vault, like his beloved mother, in a cemetery in Brooklyn, New York. His life had been one death-defying stunt after another, but even the Great Houdini could not escape the vault which would finally hold him.

PETER HERSHORNE

The snow-capped Colorado mountain was a
challenge to hot-dog ski enthusiast, Peter
Hershorne. For Peter, this slope represented an
invitation to excitement! His plan was to do the
risky double-back layout with a spread-eagle
jump!

Peter remembers leaving the mountain as his skis made a perfect takeoff. But something went wrong! The takeoff fell ten feet shorter than Peter had hoped!

A deathly silence followed as Peter lay in the snow, unconscious. A helicopter was summoned and quickly came to Peter's aid, but tragedy was to strike again. En route to the Denver hospital, the helicopter crashed! After he was removed from the wreckage, the young man was finally taken to hospital.

When Peter awoke, he thought he had lived through a horrible nightmare! He couldn't remember anything following the crash. But he would recover and soon be back on the slopes again - or so he thought.

With the numb sensation in his legs, he was completely immobilized. Doctors informed him that his spinal cord had been severed and he would never walk again. Peter did not believe that.

After four months and two unsuccessful operations, Peter still found it difficult to accept his fate. He was a young man who had a zest for life, who lived to the fullest, enthusiastically grabbing at every opportunity for excitement! How could he continue such a life as a paraplegic?

Though often frustrated, Peter persevered through a grueling physical therapy course. For the young man who could once do "anything" with ease, now even the simplest tasks became a major undertaking.

Just seventeen months following his tragic accident, however, Peter took up sailing. Harnessed to his boat to avoid toppling overboard, Peter rose to the challenge and mastered the sport. Once again, he began to feel that old stirring of excitement, and as before, his life seemed full of potential. Life wasn't over yet - not by a long shot!

After sailing, Peter took up scuba diving. He became the first paraplegic to qualify for senior scuba diving certification. Nothing could stop Peter now. Seeking out sports he might do, he decided upon kayaking. Belted and secured into his seat, Peter took a three-week, 280-mile trek through the difficult rapids of the Grand Canyon. Peter admitted he was a little worried about this expedition, but it was something he had to do - he had to know for himself that he could still face a challenge.

Competing with able-bodied athletes, Peter compiled an endless list of exploits. He had sailed a catamaran in national competition, scuba dived off Australia's Great Barrier Reef and kayaked through the most dangerous white water rapids of North America. On one kayaking excursion, Peter was swept through the entire course of the rapids upside down!

Accepting the limitations of his physical condition did not mean giving up. Though there were many things he could never do again, there were still many other things he'd never tried to do...and could. "If I thought about limitations," says Peter, "I'd still be in the hospital."

SPIDER MEN

Mount Everest and the rest of the world's highest mountains may have been conquered, but there are still a lot of buildings left to climb.

In 1983 "Spider Dan" Goodwin worked his way up the outside of the sky-scraping Sears Tower in Chicago, despite attempts by Chicago firemen to hose him down.

Another building climber is window washer Ben Colli. In the early 1980's he started a tradition. Every July 4th he jumps off the 75-story Peachtree Plaza in Atlanta, Georgia, hanging on to a rope and swinging himself down its sides in 150-200 feet swoops. It is a terrifying stunt for which the hotel owners pay him well.

Most building climbers, however, are not paid for it. In 1977, George Willig climbed the outside of the 1,350-foot high World Trade Center in New York City. The city sued him for $250,000, hoping to recover the money it spent as a result of his stunt. They had had to provide many costly city services, such as police officers who followed Willig up the side of the building in a window washer's carriage and those who arrested him at the top. Willig wound up paying a fine of only $1.10 - one cent for each of the stories he had climbed.

PONY EXPRESS

The ad in the newspaper read:

WANTED - Young skinny, wiry fellows not over 18. Must be expert riders willing to risk death. Orphans preferred.

Hundreds of young boys responded to this ad. Some were orphans - those who were not left behind grieving parents if they were one of those who lost their lives on the job.

California was almost uninhabited, but a speck of gold spotted in a riverbed ignited the widespread frenzy known as the Great California Gold Rush. As a result, California's population swelled to more than half a million. These new inhabitants longed to hear from their families still located in the East. Mail took months to arrive because it was delivered by stage coaches that criss-crossed the entire country. By the time the gold miners had word from home, the letters were at least three or four months old. There had to be a better way!

William Hepburn Russel was the man with the solution. A direct route was mapped from Missouri to the West Coast, and instead of using slow-moving stage coaches, he provided a team of speedy horses that could, Russel boasted, reach California in 10 days! This relay of horses was to become the famous "Pony Express."

One hundred and ninety stations were posted throughout the 1,800-mile western wilderness; 500 horses were put in operation, and 80 young men hired to ride with the mail across the country. These riders not only withstood the cruel elements of nature - the blistering heat, driving rain, sleet, and blizzards, through deserts and over rough mountain terrain - but they met with the threat of hostile Indians. On many occasions, the boys had to protect their mail with their lives. But the mail was finally coming through and the Californians were ecstatic!

The Pony Express operated a two-way system. When the first rider was dispatched from Missouri, another rider was leaving Sacramento, California. Relay stations were placed every five to ten miles to allow the riders a change of fresh horses - a switch that took all of two minutes! "Swing" or "home" stations were located every 50 to 100 miles where the riders ate and slept.

These riders each weighed under 130 pounds. Excess bulk would only slow the horses down. They were paid handsomely, but the dangers and hardships accompanying the job were

many. The Indian wars alone claimed the live of 17 Pony Express riders.

One young rider lived to tell the story of hi attack by the Paiute Indians of Nevada, a fierc tribe who were dreaded enemies of the "white man." The rider, named Nick Wilson, wa helping defend a station against an Indian raid He looked up to see an Indian aiming his bov and arrow directly at him! Before he had a moment to react, Wilson felt a sudden searing pain a few inches above his left eye. Bloo trickled down the side of his face. Wilson struck by the arrow, collapsed to th floor. His friends tried to pull the arrow out but the shaft came away and left the flint splin in his head. The arrow point was still lodge in his skull! His friends thought Wilson wa doomed to a tragic death, but incredibly, afte 18 days in a comatose state, Wilson regaine consciousness.

Some pony riders had to run two or three leg of the journey because their companions wer either killed or held hostage by this hostil native tribe. These riders were a dedicate group of young boys who were steadfast i their mission to get the mail through.

Even the horses were of special quality. Th ponies used were newly broken mustangs tough and fiery, but ideal for the task. Thes horses were well-trained to carry the mai through. On several occasions where rider were killed while traveling through Paiut Indian wars, the riderless horses continued t make their way to the next mail station. Pon Express riders could detect enemy India territory by simply watching the movement c their pony's ears - a sure sign of trouble ahead!

The Pony Express succeeded in capturing th hearts and imagination of all Americans. lasted for only one and a half years becaus the transcontinental telegraph system was i operation and news now could be wired fror coast to coast. On October 26, 1861, the Pon Express ceased to exist. In its short ye glamorous history, the Pony Express delivere 30,000 pieces of mail, with only one lost ma pouch!

'Blast Off'!

The 22-foot silver cannon was aimed and ready. The audience held its breath as the cannon was loaded. Then someone screamed out, "Fire!"

A thunderous boom rocked New York's Polo Grounds as Victoria Zacchini, a 110-pound girl, soared through the air. Setting a record speed of 100 miles per hour, she climbed to a height of over 100 feet and safely landed in a net 200 feet away.

Victoria is only one of a family of human cannonballs. Her father, Emanuel, broke records for the longest distance traveled from the mouth of a cannon. When he retired in 1940, Victoria took up the show.

Although many have tried this daring feat, few have succeeded. Over 30 human cannonballs have perished within this century.

Across the Atlantic

It was 1894 when two seamen, George Samuelson and Frank
Harbo, decided to make a cross-Atlantic voyage in a rowboat.
After two years of practicing their long-distance rowing
skills, they were ready to embark from the New York
Harbor.

Hundreds of cheering fans lined the shore and journalists
reported that the sailors' attempt would be nothing short of
suicide. The two daring men, however, were well prepared
and, although they assumed they would have hardships, they
saw clearly the acclaim and fortune which would await them
as celebrities when they reached the shores of Le Havre,
France.

Made of sturdy oak and cedar planks, their rowboat, which
they'd made themselves, measured 18 feet and 4 inches
long by 5 feet wide. It was stocked with 60 gallons of fresh
drinking water, a generous supply of canned goods and
oatmeal, five spare sets of oars, and a huge canvas sheet
which would protect them from storms.

They rowed for 18 hours a day, breaking only to sleep and
eat. At this rate they traveled 54 miles daily.

Five weeks passed and at this point they decided to alter
their direction for England, which would be closer.

After 56 days of hard labor at sea, the two men reached
England's coast on August 1, 1896. As there were no
waiting crowds to greet them, however, nor any fame or
fortune to come, they had to be content with just having
done it.

by Rowboat

ALBERT SCHWEITZER

Sometimes an act of courage challenges death for a fleeting moment - other times it endures hardship and sacrifice over a long period of time. Albert Schweitzer's courageous deeds, which earned him the Nobel Peace Prize in 1952, combined long-term hardship with an ever-present risk of illness, disease and death that spanned almost half a century.

By the age of 28, Schweitzer was not only a pastor, musician, doctor of philosophy, and author of many fine books on music and religion, but he had become a professor at Strasbourg University and principal of St. Thomas' College. It was a comfortable life, but, for Schweitzer, it was empty.

One evening, while deeply involved in his work, he came across a magazine that had been placed on his desk. It was a report from the Paris Missionary Society, and as he thumbed through it, he discovered an article entitled, "The Needs of the Congo Mission." He read about the African tribes of the Congo Basin, whose lives were in constant battle with the sweltering heat and spreading of disease - and Schweitzer knew what he would do.

Schweitzer was 36 years old when he wrote the final exam which qualified him to be a doctor. The following year was spent acquiring hospital experience, learning about tropical diseases and raising funds for the work he planned to do in Africa. He would build, equip and operate a hospital at his own expense. He had chosen Lambarene, on the Ogowe River, so that patients could travel quickly to the hospital by canoe.

On Good Friday, 1913, Albert and his wife, Helene - an experienced nurse - set out on their Congo mission. Their first view of Africa, the continent to which they would devote most of their lives, was not inviting. A strange town built on a steep slope wavered like a mirage in the intense heat. Its streets were cracked, rutted, and steaming from the sun's rays. From here they would travel overland and by river until they reached their 4-room wooden house near their mission. This small, cramped house with its dark dampness, the home of cockroaches and spiders, seemed to the Schweitzers like some horrible, nightmarish prison cell.

News of the Schweitzers' arrival spread like wildfire through the forest. Even before their crates of supplies had arrived, dozens of patients crowded around their house. These people were the wild nomads of the forest. They were as helpless and uncomplaining as animals in suffering. One old leper held out the stump of an arm, wrapped in filthy rags; his wife had paddled their canoe more than 200 miles to reach them. A baby cried in its mother's arms; the infant's body was red raw and smeared with blood. Another, a woman, trembled with malaria. These desolate faces turned their hallowed eyes to Albert – with love.

An abandoned chicken coop was made into a hospital and supply hut, and in the first nine months, Albert and Helene treated more than 2,000 people. But the harsh environment made their work never ending. Poisonous snakes nested in the undergrowth and crocodiles basked, half-hidden, in the sandbanks of the river. Mosquitoes carried the germs of malaria and tsetse flies spread the dangerous "sleeping sickness." Some nights, at the beginning and end of the rainy season, traveler ants covered the hospital floor in a quivering, black mass.

In 1917, because of the First World War, the Schweitzers were forced to return to France. By this time both Albert and Helene were suffering the effects of overwork and exposure to disease; as well, Helene was expecting a child. When Albert did return to Africa two years later, Helene and their daughter remained behind.

The old hospital was all but swallowed up by the rain forests. Schweitzer cleaned it up and made it operational again, but it was still in a sorry state. Finally, the French government lent him a hand by granting him 172 acres of land. By July, 1927 this land housed a large new hospital, around which grew "a Garden of Eden."

As the years passed, the hospital grew, and Schweitzer continued in the face of his weariness. On September 4, 1965, Albert Schweitzer died in the African village of Lambarene, where he was buried. Earlier, he'd written, "Life becomes harder for me in every way, than it would be if I lived for myself alone, but at the same time it becomes richer more beautiful and happier. It becomes instead of mere living, a real experience of life."